Ocean Exploration

Rebecca L. Johnson

PICTURE CREDITS

Cover, Photographer's Choice/Getty Images; 1, 31 (center left), Darrell Gulin/Corbis; pages 2-3, 7 (top right), Royalty-Free/Corbis; pages 4-5, 34 (second from bottom), Reuters/Corbis; pages 6-7, 30 (top left), Stone/Getty Images; pages 9 (top right), 29 (bottom right), 31 (top left), Photodisc Green/Getty Images; page 9 (bottom right), Taxi/Getty Images; pages 11 (left), 31 (bottom right), Ralph A. Clevenger/Corbis; pages 11 (right), 15, 34 (top), 35 (bottom), E. Widder/HBOI/Visuals Unlimited; pages 12, 34 (bottom), Amos Nachoum/Corbis; pages 13, 31 (top right), 35 (center), Alexis Rosenfeld/Photo Researchers, Inc.; pages 14, 25 (bottom left), 35 (top), Gary Bell/Australian Picture Library/Corbis; pages 16-17, David Wrobel/SeaPics.com; pages 18, 23, 30 (bottom left), Emory Kristof/National Geographic Image Collection; pages 20 (bottom left), 25 (bottom center), 31 (center right), 34 (second from top), Dave Wrobel/MBARI; pages 20-21 (center), 30 (top right), David French/MBARI 1996; page 21, Kim Reisenbichler/1996 MBARI; page 22, Copyright 2002 MBARI; page 25 (bottom right), Ralph White/Corbis; pages 26, 31 (bottom left), Courtesy of the Institute for Exploration, Mystic, Connecticut; page 27, The Image Bank/Getty Images; pages 28, 30 (bottom right), Chinch Gryniewicz, Ecoscene/Corbis; page 29 (top), Douglas Faulkner/Photo Researchers, Inc.; page 32, Ralph A. Clevenger/Corbis; page 36, Ingram Publishing.

Produced through the worldwide resources of the National Geographic Society, John M. Fahey, Jr., President and Chief Executive Officer; Gilbert M. Grosvenor, Chairman of the Board; Nina D. Hoffman, Executive Vice President and President, Books and Education Publishing Group.

PREPARED BY NATIONAL GEOGRAPHIC SCHOOL PUBLISHING

Ericka Markman, Senior Vice President and President, Children's Books and Education Publishing Group; Steve Mico, Senior Vice President, Editorial Director, Publisher; Francis Downey, Executive Editor; Richard Easby, Editorial Manager; Bea Jackson, Director of Layout and Design; Jim Hiscott, Design Manager; Cynthia Olson, Art Director; Margaret Sidlosky, Illustrations Director; Matt Wascavage, Manager of Publishing Services; Sean Philpotts, Jane Ponton, Production Managers; Ted Tucker, Production Specialist.

MANUFACTURING AND QUALITY CONTROL

Christopher A. Liedel, Chief Financial Officer; Phillip L. Schlosser, Director; Clifton M. Brown III, Manager

BOOK DEVELOPMENT

Amy Sarver

BOOK DESIGN/PHOTO RESEARCH

3R1 Group, Inc.

◀ **People use scuba gear and other tools to explore the ocean.**

Contents

Copyright © 2006 National Geographic Society.
All Rights Reserved. Reproduction of the whole or any part of the
contents without written permission from the publisher is prohibited.
National Geographic, National Geographic School Publishing,
National Geographic Reading Expeditions, and the Yellow Border
are registered trademarks of the National Geographic Society.

Published by the National Geographic Society
1145 17th Street N.W.
Washington, D.C. 20036-4688

ISBN-13: 978-0-7922-5430-0
ISBN-10: 0-7922-5430-9

Fifth Printing May 2016

Printed in Canada.

The Water Planet

From outer space, Earth looks like a huge marble. The green and brown areas are land. The white swirls are clouds. The blue is water in the **ocean.**

The ocean is the large area of water that covers most of Earth's surface. The ocean is deep. It is also full of life. The ocean is home to many of Earth's living things.

Look at the picture and chart.
- What does the picture show?
- What does the chart show?
- Why is the ocean an important part of Earth's surface?

....

ocean – the large area of water that covers most of Earth's surface

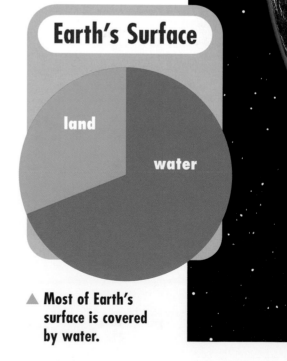

Earth's Surface

land

water

▲ Most of Earth's surface is covered by water.

water

land

clouds

▲ From outer space, you can see Earth's clouds, land, and water.

Big Idea

The ocean covers most of Earth's surface and is home to many kinds of living things.

Set Purpose

Learn about the ocean and how scientists explore it.

How Do Peo
Explore th

Questions You Will Explore

What are some features of the ocean?

How do scientists explore the ocean?

...ple ...e Ocean?

▲ From under the water, people can see many kinds of living things.

What do you see when you look at the ocean from above? Waves hit the shore. Birds dive into the ocean water. But mostly the ocean looks big and blue.

What would you see if you looked below the surface? You would see many kinds of living things.

How do we know about ocean life? People have made tools to study the ocean and the living things within it.

▲ From above, the ocean looks big and blue.

Areas of the Ocean

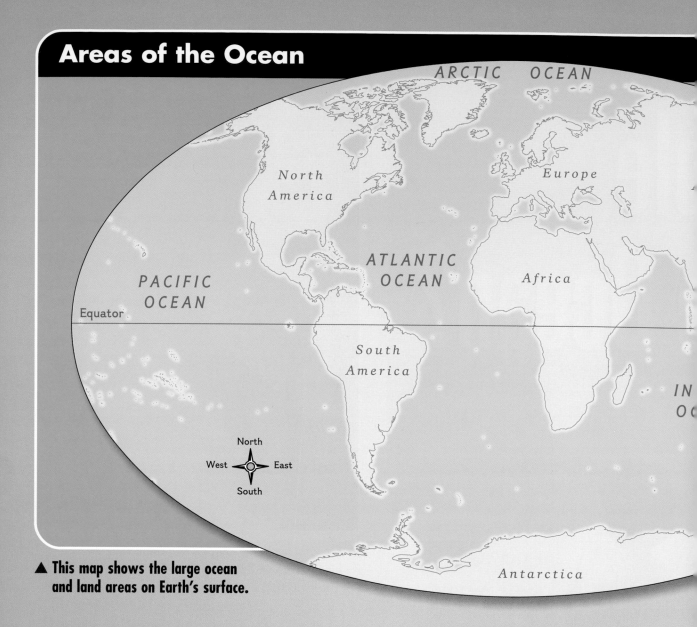

ARCTIC OCEAN

North America

Europe

ATLANTIC OCEAN

Africa

PACIFIC OCEAN

Equator

South America

IN
O

North

West — East

South

Antarctica

▲ This map shows the large ocean and land areas on Earth's surface.

The Planet's Ocean

The ocean is very big. People have given names to different areas of the ocean. The largest areas are called the Pacific Ocean, Atlantic Ocean, Indian Ocean, and Arctic Ocean. The map above shows these ocean areas.

Ocean Sizes

Ocean	Size (in square kilometers)
Pacific Ocean	165,250,000
Atlantic Ocean	82,440,000
Indian Ocean	73,440,000
Arctic Ocean	5,106,000

▲ Earth's coldest water is found in the Arctic Ocean.

▲ Earth's warmest ocean water is near the Equator.

Ocean Water

Some areas of the ocean are colder than others.
The Arctic Ocean is the most northern ocean
area. It has Earth's coldest water. The Pacific,
Atlantic, and Indian Oceans are farther south.
The water in these ocean areas is warmer than
in the Arctic. The warmest ocean water is near
the **Equator.**

Equator — the area around the planet halfway between Earth's
most northern and southern points

Ocean Depths

▲ Ocean water is shallow near the shoreline and deep in trenches.

Ocean Depths

Some parts of the ocean are deeper than others. The place where the ocean meets the land is called the **shoreline**. Near the shoreline, the ocean is usually not very deep.

The deepest parts of the ocean are in **trenches**. A trench is a long, narrow valley in the ocean floor. The deepest trench is in the Pacific Ocean. It is more than 10,800 meters (36,000 feet) deep.

....

shoreline – the place where ocean water meets the land

trench – a long, narrow valley in the ocean floor

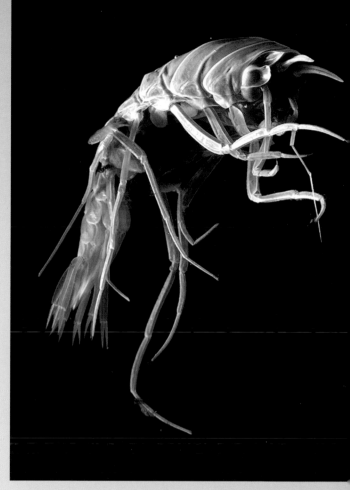

▲ These plants live in shallow water. Here, the water pressure is not very great.

▲ This animal lives in deep water. Here, the water pressure is much greater.

Life Under Pressure

In all parts of the ocean, there is **water pressure**. Water pressure is the weight of water on objects and living things. This weight becomes heavier the deeper the water gets.

Most living things in the ocean are found in **shallow** water. Here, the water pressure is not very great. Fewer animals live in deep ocean water. Their bodies must be able to withstand more water pressure.

....

water pressure – the weight of water on objects or living things

shallow – not deep

mask

air tank

▲ Scuba gear lets people explore shallow areas of the ocean.

Ocean Zones

Scientists study living things in ocean water. They find out what lives in different layers, or zones, of the ocean.

Each zone is at a different depth in the ocean. The sunlight zone is the top layer of the ocean. Below the sunlight zone is the twilight zone. The midnight zone is next. The **abyssal** zone is the bottom, or deepest, layer of the ocean.

....

abyssal – having to do with the deepest area of the ocean

▶ Each ocean zone is at a different depth.

Ocean Zones

sunlight zone
twilight zone

midnight zone

abyssal zone

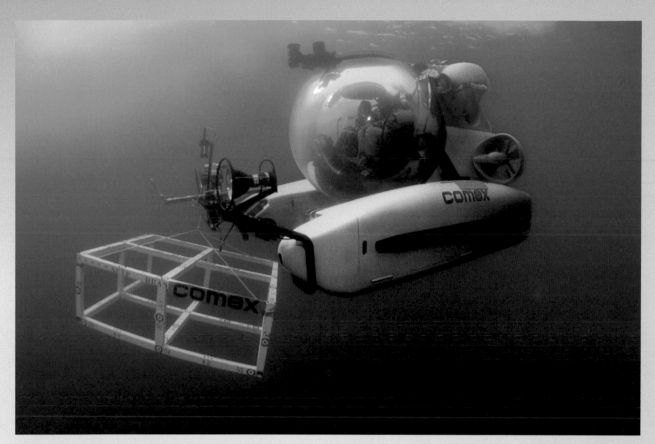

▲ **A submersible helps people explore deep areas of the ocean.**

Ocean Tools

How do people learn about life in each zone? They use special tools. In shallow parts of the ocean, people can use **scuba** gear. Scuba gear is equipment attached to a tank of air. Scuba gear lets people breathe underwater.

People cannot swim deep down in the ocean. So they explore the deep ocean with tools such as **submersibles.** Submersibles are small boats that travel underwater. They are strong. Their walls can withstand the great pressure of deep water.

scuba – equipment connected to an air tank that lets a person breathe underwater

submersible – a small boat that can travel in deep ocean water

▲ **Many kinds of animals and plants live in the sunlight zone.**

Life in Sunlight

What have scientists learned about the ocean zones? The sunlight zone stretches down to about 200 meters (660 feet). That is as deep as most of the sun's rays can reach.

Ocean plants grow in the sunlight zone. This is because plants have enough light from the sun to grow. Thousands of kinds of fish live in this zone. Other kinds of animals live here, too. The sunlight zone is home to more kinds of living things than all of the other ocean zones put together.

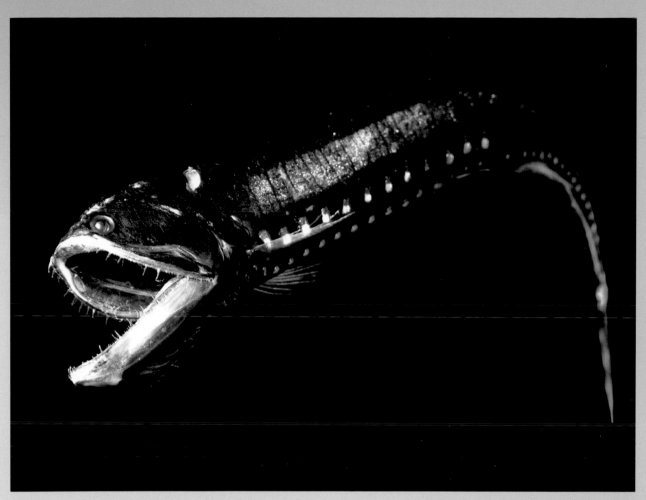

▲ **This fish lives in deep ocean water.**

Deeper and Darker

Below the sunlight and twilight zones, the ocean is dark. Sunlight cannot travel this far down. So fewer kinds of living things are found in deeper ocean zones. Plants do not grow in these zones. Yet some kinds of animals live in the deep, dark ocean.

Different kinds of living things live at different depths of the ocean. Each day, scientists learn more about the ocean and ocean life.

Stop and Think!

How do scientists study the different ocean zones?

Recap
Explain how scientists explore different parts of the ocean.

Set Purpose
Learn how scientists use a robot submersible to explore the deep ocean.

Dive

Into the

A strange creature floats through deep ocean water. Its body is covered with long, wavy feelers called tentacles. What is this strange animal? It is a type of jellyfish. This jellyfish lives in deep ocean water. People cannot swim in water this deep. So how do we know the jellyfish is there? A robot submersible shows us.

▶ A deep-sea jellyfish

Deep

Seeing Into the Deep

The robot submersible is named *Tiburon*. *Tiburon* travels through deep ocean water. But this submersible does not carry people. *Tiburon* is controlled by a pilot on a ship above.

Tiburon has many tools. It has lights and cameras. It also has tools for catching ocean animals. *Tiburon* can bring animals back to the ship. Then scientists can study them.

▲ *Tiburon* lets scientists see animals in deep ocean water.

Exploring the Deep Ocean

Tiburon can travel down to 3,600 meters (12,000 feet). Scientists use it to explore deep parts of the ocean. For example, they explore Monterey Canyon.

Monterey Canyon begins just off the coast of California. It is about 160 kilometers (100 miles) long. In places, the canyon is nearly 3,500 meters (11,500 feet) deep. That is more than two miles down!

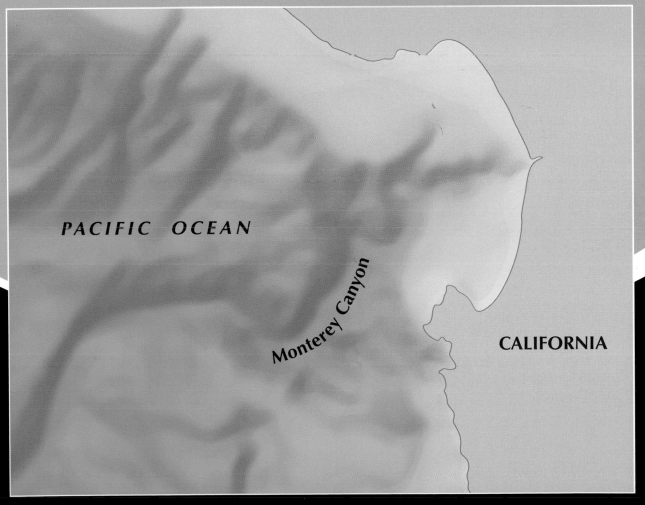

PACIFIC OCEAN

Monterey Canyon

CALIFORNIA

▲ *Tiburon* can explore very deep areas of the Monterey Canyon.

Light Show

Tiburon helps scientists study animals in Monterey Canyon. *Tiburon* takes pictures of animals in the deep ocean water. Most of these animals have body parts that glow. The glow is called **bioluminescence**. It is light that the animals make in their bodies. These animals put on a light show in the dark underwater world.

....

bioluminescence – a light made by living things

▼ **Cameras on *Tiburon* let scientists see many deep-sea animals.**

▶ **This jellyfish has body parts that glow.**

Disappearing Act

Tiburon sends pictures of ocean animals back to the ship. A scientist looks at the pictures on a video screen. The scientist sees a jellyfish swim by. The jellyfish glows as it moves through the water.

Soon, the scientist sees other deep-sea animals. A vampire squid appears. The pilot makes *Tiburon* turn. This motion scares the squid. The squid pulls its arms up over its body. This helps protect the squid from danger.

▼ The vampire squid can pull its arms over its head when it is scared.

arms ▷

What Are You?

The pilot guides *Tiburon* deeper and deeper. Something new comes into sight. It has a white body with moving parts. The scientist is very excited. He has only seen this animal a few times before. He wants to learn more about it.

▼ Scientists want to learn more about this deep-sea animal.

Back Onboard

The pilot moves *Tiburon* closer. *Tiburon* gently pulls the animal into a tank. Then *Tiburon* returns to the ship. Scientists raise *Tiburon* out of the water. They take the animal to the ship's laboratory. There they will study it closely. Exploring ocean life is exciting work!

Stop and Think!

How does *Tiburon* help scientists learn about the ocean?

▲ On the ship, scientists raise *Tiburon* out of the water.

Recap

Explain how robot submersibles help scientists study the deep ocean.

Set Purpose

Read these articles to learn more about the ocean and ocean exploration.

Earth's Ocean

The ocean covers most of Earth's surface. It is home to many kinds of living things. Here are some ideas you learned about the ocean.

- The largest areas of the ocean are the Pacific Ocean, Atlantic Ocean, Indian Ocean, and Arctic Ocean.
- Many kinds of plants and animals live in the ocean's sunlight zone.
- Fewer kinds of animals live in deeper parts of the ocean.
- Scientists use tools to explore the ocean.

Check What You Have Learned

What do the map and photos show about the ocean?

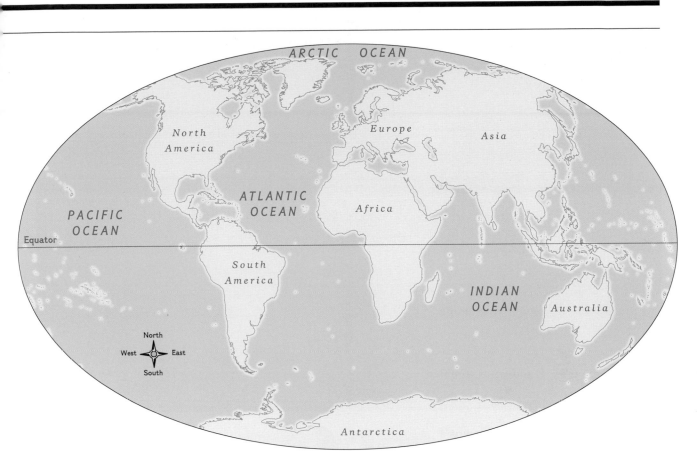

▲ This map shows large areas of the ocean.

▲ The sunlight zone is home to many kinds of living things.

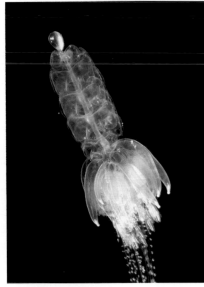

▲ This jellyfish lives in deep ocean water.

▲ A submersible lets scientists study living things in deep ocean water.

▲ *Hercules* is a robot submersible that explores shipwrecks.

Searching for Shipwrecks

Some ocean explorers discover new ocean animals. Others discover sunken ships. For example, Robert Ballard looks for old shipwrecks. A robot submersible called *Hercules* helps him search.

Hercules can explore shipwrecks. It can brush sand and dirt off objects in the water. *Hercules* can pick up these objects and carry them safely to the surface.

Life on a Reef

Coral reefs are home to many kinds of living things. A reef is like stone. It is made of the skeletons of tiny coral animals. Living coral builds on the dead parts of other coral.

Coral reefs are found where ocean water is warm, shallow, and clear. The largest coral reef is the Great Barrier Reef. This reef runs for 2,010 kilometers (1,250 miles). It is found along Australia's east coast.

▼ **Coral reefs are home to many kinds of living things.**

Oil in the Ocean

Each year, a lot of oil ends up in the ocean. Oil can kill things living in the ocean. How does oil get into the ocean? Some seeps, or flows, from rocks on the ocean floor. Oil that people use can end up washing into the ocean. Some oil gets into the ocean when people move oil from one place to another. Oil can also get in the ocean when people try to take it from rocks on the ocean floor.

▼ These people carefully clean up oil that spilled into the ocean.

▲ Marine sanctuaries protect areas of the ocean where these manatees live.

Marine Sanctuaries

In 1972, the United States Congress made laws to protect the ocean. Some laws protect areas of the ocean called marine sanctuaries. *Marine* means "of the sea." *Sanctuary* means "a protected area." So marine sanctuaries are protected areas of the sea, or ocean.

▶ Marine sanctuaries also help birds and other animals.

Today, there are thirteen national marine sanctuaries. They are in the Pacific and Atlantic Oceans. They include places where many ocean animals live and have babies. Some sanctuaries protect forests of underwater plants.

29

Many kinds of words are used in this book. Here you will learn about adverbs. You will also learn about adjectives.

Adverbs

Adverbs are words that describe a verb, adjective, or another adverb. An adverb tells when, how, or how much. Find the adverbs below. What does each adverb describe?

The ocean is **very** big.

The submersible can **safely** bring objects back to the ship.

The scientist looks **closely** at the computer screen.

The people **carefully** clean oil from a beach.

Adjectives

Adjectives are words that describe people, places, or things. Find the adjectives below. What does each adjective describe?

Earth's **coldest** water is in the Arctic Ocean.

Submersibles can explore **deep** parts of the ocean.

The sea star lives in **shallow** water.

This animal lights up in **dark** water.

Robert Ballard searches for **ancient** ships.

Some marine sanctuaries protect **underwater** plants.

Research and Write

Write About an Ocean Zone

Research a zone of the ocean. Find out what kinds of animals live there. Make a poster telling what you learned.

Research

Collect books and reference materials, or go online.

Read and Take Notes

As you read, take notes and draw pictures.

Write

Make a poster that shows information about the ocean zone that you chose. Draw pictures of the animals that live there. Write a paragraph that tells what life is like in the zone.

Read and Compare

Read More About the Ocean

Find and read other books about the ocean. As you read, think about these questions.

- Why is the ocean important to life on Earth?
- What kinds of living things are found in the ocean?
- How do scientists study the ocean?

Books to Read

▲ Read about the ocean and the life within it.

▲ Read about the water on Earth.

▲ Read about the ocean and life along its shore.

Glossary

abyssal (page 12)
Having to do with the deepest area of the ocean
No sunlight reaches the abyssal zone.

bioluminescence (page 20)
A light made by living things
The glow of the squid is bioluminescence.

Equator (page 9)
The area around the planet halfway between Earth's most northern and southern points
Earth's warmest ocean water is near the Equator.

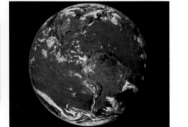

ocean (page 4)
The large area of water that covers most of Earth's surface
Earth's ocean can be seen from space.

scuba (page 13)
Equipment connected to an air tank that lets a person breathe underwater
The diver breathes with the help of scuba gear.

KEY CONCEPT

shallow (page 11)
Not deep
Coral reefs are found in shallow water.

KEY CONCEPT

shoreline (page 10)
The place where ocean water meets the land
The water at the shoreline is often shallow.

KEY CONCEPT

submersible (page 13)
A small boat that can travel in deep ocean water
The submersible explores deep below the ocean's surface.

KEY CONCEPT

trench (page 10)
A long, narrow valley in the ocean floor
The trench is deep in the ocean.

KEY CONCEPT

KEY CONCEPT

water pressure (page 11)
The weight of water on objects or living things
This animal's body can stand the water pressure
in the deep ocean.

Index